Unitarianism

W. G. Tarrant

UNITARIANISM

W. G. TARRANT

LONDON

1912

CONTENTS

INTRODUCTION

In certain quiet nooks of Old England, and, by contrast, in some of the busiest centres of New England, landmarks of religious history are to be found which are not to be easily understood by every passer-by. He is familiar with the ordinary places of worship, at least as features in, the picture of town or village. Here is the parish church where the English episcopal order has succeeded to the Roman; yonder is the more modern dissenting chapel, homely or ornate. But, now and then, among the non-episcopal buildings we find what is called distinctively a 'Meeting House, ' or more briefly a 'Meeting, ' which may perhaps be styled 'Old, ' 'New, ' or 'Great'. Its architecture usually corresponds with the simplicity of its name. Plain almost to ugliness, yet not without some degree of severe dignity, stand these old barn-like structures of brick—occasionally of stone; bearing the mellowing touch of time, surrounded by a little overshadowed graveyard, they often add a peculiar quaintness and solemnity to the scene. Mrs. Gaskell has described one such in her novel *Ruth*, and admirers of her art should know well that her own grave lies beside the little sanctuary she pictured so lovingly.

Sometimes, however, the surroundings of the ancient chapel are less attractive. It stands, it may be, in some poverty-stricken corner or court of a town or city. Whatever picturesqueness it may have had once has long since vanished. Unlovely decay, an air of desolation, symptoms of neglect, present a mournful sight, and one wonders how much longer the poor relic will remain. Many places of the kind have already been swept away; others have been renovated, enlarged, and kept more worthy of their use. Not all the Meeting Houses are of one kind. Independents, Baptists, and Friends, each possess some of them. Now and again the notice-board tells us that this is a 'Presbyterian' place of worship, but a loyal Scot who yearns for an echo of the kirk would be greatly surprised on finding, as he would if he entered, that the doctrine and worship there is not Calvinistic in any shape whatever, but—*Unitarian*.

A similar surprise awaits the visitor to New England, it may be even a greater. For if he should tread In the footsteps of the Pilgrim Fathers and find the 'lineal descendants' of their original places of worship at Plymouth, Salem, or Boston, he will find *Unitarians* in possession. So it is in many of the oldest towns founded by the American colonists of the seventeenth century. In their centres the parish churches, 'First, ' 'Second, ' or otherwise, stand forth challenging everybody's attention. There is no lack of self-assertion here, nothing at all like the shrinking of the Old English Presbyterian into obscure alleys and corners. Spacious, well appointed, and secure, these *Unitarian* parish churches, in the words of a popular Unitarian poet, 'look the whole world in the face, and fear not any man. '

The object of the present brief sketch is to show how these landmarks have come to be where they are, to trace the thoughts and fortunes of Unitarians from their rise in modern times, to indicate their religious temper and practical aims, and to exhibit the connections of the English-speaking Unitarians with some closely approximating groups in Europe and Asia.

Before entering upon a story which is extremely varied and comprehensive, one or two important points must be emphasized. In the first place the reader must bear in mind that the term 'Unitarianism' is one of popular application. It has not been chosen and imposed as sect-name by any sect-founder, or by any authoritative assembly. There has never been a leader or a central council whose decisions on these matters have been, accepted by Unitarians as final. Even when most closely organized they have steadily resisted all attempts so to fix the meaning of 'Unitarianism' as to exclude further growth of opinion. Consequently there is always room for variety of opinion among them; and every statement of their principles and teachings must be taken as a sort of average estimated from a survey more or less extended.

Thus the significance of Unitarianism as a feature of modern religious development cannot be grasped apart from its history as a movement of thought. Nowhere is it more necessary than here to reflect that to know what a thing is we must know what it has been and consider what its future naturally involves.

Secondly, amid all the varieties of thought referred to, complicated as they are by the eager advance of some and the clinging to survivals by others, there are two notes to be found undeniably, if unequally, characteristic of Unitarianism. It is both *rationalist* and *mystical*. If the historian seems more attentive to the former than to the latter, this must not be taken as indicating their relative importance. Obviously, it is easier to record controversies than to unfold the wealth of profound conceptions. Perhaps we may fairly suggest the true state of the case by the mere juxtaposition of such earlier names as Socinus, Bidle, and Locke, with those of Channing, Emerson, and Martineau; or by a reference to the earlier Unitarian hymns in contrast with those of the later stages.

SOME TERMS EXPLAINED

A brief explanation at the outset may help the reader to follow more intelligently the history of Unitarianism. As is well known, the chief issue between Trinitarians and Unitarians arises in connection with the relation of Jesus Christ to God, questions concerning the Holy Spirit being usually less discussed. There are consequential issues also, bearing upon man's nature, atonement, salvation, and other subjects, but these call for no remark here. In its full statement, as given for instance in the 'Athanasian Creed, ' the Trinitarian dogma presents the conception of Three 'Persons' in One God—Father, Son, and Holy Spirit—'Persons' with different: functions, but all equal and co-eternal. The Eastern (Greek Orthodox) Church differs from the Western (Roman Catholic) in holding that the Third Person 'proceeds' from the Father alone; the Western adds—'and from the Son' (*filioque*). The full dogma as given in the 'Athanasian Creed' is not thought to be earlier than the fifth century; debates as to the 'two natures' in Christ, and the 'two wills, ' and other abstruse points involved in the dogma, continued for centuries still. At an earlier period discussion was carried on as to whether the Son were of the 'same substance' (*homo-ousion*) or 'similar substance' (*homoi-ousion*) with the Father. The latter view was held by Arius and his party at the Council of Nicaea, A.D. 325. Athanasius held the former view, which in time, but only after many years of controversial strife and actual warfare, became established as orthodox. The Arians regarded the Son, as a subordinate being, though still divine. Another variety of opinion was put forth by Sabellius (*c.* 250 A. D.), who took the different Persons to be so many diverse modes or manifestations of the One God. This Sabellian idea, though officially condemned, has been often held in later times. Socinianism, so far as regards the personality and rank of Christ, differed from Arianism, which maintained his pre-existence, though not eternal; the Socinian doctrine being that the man Jesus was raised by God's approving benignity to 'divine' rank, and that he thus became a fit object of Christian 'worship. ' The Humanitarian view, finally, presented Jesus as a 'mere man, ' i. e. a being not essentially different in his nature from the rest of humankind. Modern Unitarianism, however, usually avoids this kind of phrase; 'all minds, ' said Channing, 'are of one family. '

THE EARLIER MOVEMENT IN ENGLAND

I. THE UNITARIAN MARTYRS

The rise of any considerable body of opinion opposed to the cardinal dogma of orthodoxy was preceded in England by a very strongly marked effort to secure liberty of thought, and a corresponding plea for a broadly comprehensive religious fellowship. The culmination of this effort, is reached, for the period first, to be reviewed, in the writings of *John Locke* (1632-1704). This celebrated man, by his powerful arguments for religious toleration and his defence of the 'reasonableness' of the Christian religion, exerted an influence of the most important kind. But we must reach him by the path of his predecessors in the same line. The principles of liberty of thought and the broadest religious fellowship are warmly espoused by Unitarians, and they look upon all who have advanced these principles as in spirit related to them, however different their respective theological conclusions may have been.

At the time of the Reformation a great deal of speculation broke forth on points hitherto closed by the Church's authority, including the fundamental doctrine of the Trinity. But, while this new ferment led to departures from the received opinions in many countries, especially in Poland and the Netherlands, the Protestant leaders maintained that upon the great articles of the creeds they were still one with Rome, and in fact they soon displayed an eagerness to stifle heresy. Men often fail to see the logic of their own position, and many who claimed the right to differ from Rome on points which Rome considered vital were unable to grant that others had an equal right to differ from Luther, Calvin, or an English State Church. The outrageous cruelty of Calvin towards the Anti-trinitarian *Servetus*, whom he caused to be burned at Geneva in 1553, affords a glaring instance of this inconsistency. But a sad proof is given that, about that time, even Anti-trinitarians themselves were not always tolerant.

Among the countries where the orthodox dogma was most freely questioned was Transylvania, adjacent to Hungary proper.

Here the sovereign, John Sigismund, took sides with the Anti-trinitarians, and issued in 1568 an edict permitting four recognized types of doctrine and worship—Romanist, Lutheran, Calvinist, and

Unitarian. The Transylvanians were at this time largely under the influence of their Polish brethren in the faith, who still practised the invocation of Christ. *Francis David*, a powerful religious leader in Hungary, having arrived at a 'Humanitarian' view of Christ two centuries before it was held by English Unitarians, opposed Christ-worship. In 1579, when a Catholic had succeeded to the throne, David was denounced for an intolerable heretic by the Polish party, and, being imprisoned, died the same year. This blot on the record has long been deplored, and David is held in honour as a martyr by the Transylvanian Unitarian Church, which still flourishes, and forms a third member in alliance with the Unitarians of Great Britain and America. As, however, these Transylvanian (popularly called 'Hungarian') Unitarians had until the nineteenth century little or no connection with the English and Americans, and have not materially affected the development of the movement, we omit the details of their special history.

In England a number of Anti-trinitarians suffered burning in the sixteenth century, being usually, but loosely, described as 'Arians. ' The last two in England who died by fire as heretics were men of this class. In March, 1612, Bartholomew Legate was burned at Smithfield, and a month later Edward Wightman had the same fate at Lichfield. So late as 1697 a youth named Pakenham was hanged at Edinburgh on the charge of heretical blasphemy. Although these were the only executions of the kind here in the seventeenth century, the evidence is but too clear that the authorities conceived it to be their duty to put down this form of opinion with the severest rigour. In a letter sent by Archbishop Neile, of York, to Bishop Laud, in 1639, reference is made to Wightman's case, and it is stated that another man, one Trendall, deserves the same sentence. A few years later, Paul Best, a scholarly gentleman who had travelled in Poland and Transylvania and there adopted Anti-trinitarian views, was sentenced by vote of the House of Commons to be hanged for denying the Trinity. The Ordinance drawn up in 1648 by the Puritan authorities was incredibly vindictive against what they judged to be heretical. Happily, Oliver Cromwell and his Independents were conscious of considerable variety of opinion in their own ranks, and apparently the Protector secured Best's liberation. It was certainly he who saved another and more memorable Unitarian from the extreme penalty.

This man was *John Bidle*, a clergyman and schoolmaster of Gloucester. His Biblical studies led him to a denial of the Trinity, which he lost no occasion of making public. During twenty years, broken by five or six imprisonments, he persisted in the effort to diffuse Unitarian teachings, and even to organize services for Unitarian worship. His writings and personal influence were so widely recognized that it became a fashion later to speak of Unitarians as 'Bidellians. ' Cromwell was evidently troubled about him, feeling repugnance to his doctrine yet averse to ill-treat a man of unblemished character. In 1655, ten years after Bidle's first imprisonment, the Protector sent him to the Scilly Islands, obviously to spare him a worse fate, and allowed him a yearly sum for maintenance. A few months before Cromwell's death, he was brought back to London, and on being set at liberty at once renewed his efforts. Finally, he was caught 'conventicling' in 1662 and sent to gaol, and in September of that year he died.

II. INFLUENCES MAKING FOR 'LATITUDE'

The foregoing sufficiently illustrates the position confronting those who at that time openly avowed their departure from the Trinitarian dogma. Those who dared and suffered were no doubt but a few of those who really shared in the heretical view; the testimony of orthodox writers is all in support of this surmise. Equally clear is the fact that while the religious authorities were thus rigorous a steadily deepening undercurrent of opinion made for 'Latitude. ' How far this Latitude might properly go was a troublesome question, but at any rate some were willing to advocate what many must have silently desired.

Apart from the extremists in the great struggle between High Church and Puritans there existed a group of moderate men, often of shrewd intellect, ripe scholarship, and attractive temper, who sought in a wider liberty of opinion an escape from the tyrannical alternatives presented by the two opposing parties. Even in connection with these very parties there were tendencies peculiar to themselves, which could not fail in the end to mitigate the force of their own contentions. The High Church was mostly 'Arminian, ' i. e. on the side of the more 'reasonable' theology of that age. The Puritans were wholly committed to the principle of democratic liberty, as then understood, and in religious matters set the Bible in the highest place of authority. It could not be but that these several factors should ultimately tell upon the solution of the problem of religious liberty. But the immediate steps toward that solution had to be taken by the advocates of Latitude. Among them were Lord Falkland, John Hales, and William Chillingworth, the last of whom is famous for his unflinching protest that 'the Bible, the Bible only, is the religion of Protestants, ' a saying which was as good as a charter to those who based their so-called heresies on the explicit words of Scripture. In the second half of that seventeenth century the work of broadening the religious mind was carried forward by others of equal or even greater ability; it is sufficient here to name Jeremy Taylor among Churchmen, and Richard Baxter among Nonconformists.

There was, of course, a good deal of levity, the temper of the Gallio who cares for none of these things. But this was not the temper of the men to whom we refer. Their greatest difficulty, indeed, arose from their intense interest in religious truth. They could not conceive a

State which should not control men's theology in some real way. Even Locke did not advocate toleration for the atheist, for such a man (in his opinion) could not make the solemn asseverations on which alone civil life could go forward. Nor would he tolerate the Roman Catholic, but in this case political considerations swayed the balance; the Catholic introduced the fatal principle of allegiance to a 'foreign prince. ' Taking for granted, then, the necessity for some degree of State supervision of religion, how could this be rendered least inimical to the general desire for liberty?

The reply to this question brought them very close to the position taken up by *Faustus Socinus* long before, viz. that the 'essentials' of a Christian faith should be recognized as few and, as far as possible, simple. Of course, it is from his name that the term 'Socinian' is derived, a term that has often been applied, but mistakenly, to Unitarians generally. The repeated and often bitter accusation brought against the advocates of Latitude that they were 'Socinians, ' or at least tainted with 'Socinianism, ' renders appropriate some short account of Socinus himself.

This man was one of the sixteenth-century Italian Reformers who were speedily crushed or dispersed by the vigilance of the Inquisition. Those who escaped wandered far, and some were at different times members of the Church for 'Strangers, ' or foreigners, to which Edward VI assigned the nave of the great Augustine Church, still standing at Austin Friars in the heart of the City of London. It is Interesting to observe here that a Dutch liberal congregation lineally inherits the place to-day. Careful investigation has shown that among the refugees here in the sixteenth century were some whose opinions were unsound on the Trinity; possibly they affected English opinion in some small degree. *Loelius Socinus* (1525-62), uncle of *Faustus* (1539-1604), was for a short time in London, but interesting thinker as he was, his nephew who never set foot in England really exerted much more influence upon English thought.

It was, however, in Poland especially that the influence of Faustus Socinus first became prominent. That country, then flourishing under its own princes, early became (as we have seen) the home of an Anti-trinitarian form of Protestantism. Socinus joined this group, and during the latter half of the sixteenth century effected much improvement among them, organizing their congregations, establishing schools, promoting a Unitarian literature. The educational work thus begun achieved great success; but in his own lifetime Socinus met with fierce opposition and even personal violence. He died in 1604; the Polish Unitarian Church fell under the persecution of both Catholics and orthodox Protestants, and was finally crushed out in 1660.

Important for our present study is the fact that the literary output of these Polish Socinians was both large and of high quality. Their 'Racovian Catechism' was translated into different languages, and early found its way into England. James I promptly had it burned, despite the fact that the Latin version was dedicated to himself! Other books and pamphlets followed, and even if we abate something as due to the exaggerating fears and suspicions of the authorities, there would seem to have been no time as the seventeenth century went on when Socinian literature was not widely circulated here, albeit at first in secret.

Into the details of this literature there is no need to go; it is sufficient to observe its outstanding features. They correspond in the main to the temper of the master mind, Socinus, a man who in the absence of imaginative genius displayed remarkable talent as a reasoner, and a liberal disposition considerably in advance of his times. The later Socinian writings, preserved in eight large volumes issued by the 'Polish Brethren' (Amsterdam, 1666), exhibit in addition the results of much diligent research and scholarship, in which the wide variety of opinion actually held by the Fathers and later Church authorities is proved, and the moral is drawn. In the presence of so much fluctuating teaching upon the abstruser points of the creeds was it not desirable to abandon the pretence of a rounded system complete in every detail? Would it not be better to simplify the faith—in other and familiar words, to reduce the number of 'essentials'? In order to discover these essentials, surely the inquirer must turn to the Bible, the record of that miraculous revelation which was given to deliver man's unassisted reason from the perils of ignorance and doubt. At the same time, man's reason itself was a divine gift, and the Bible should be carefully and rationally studied in order to gather its real message. As the fruit of such study the Socinians not only propounded an Anti-trinitarian doctrine derived from Scripture, but in particular emphasized the arguments against the substitutionary atonement as presented in the popular Augustinian scheme and philosophically expounded in Anselm's *Cur Deus Homo*. Socinus himself must be credited with whatever force belongs to these criticisms on the usual doctrine of the death of Christ, and it may be fairly said that most of the objections advanced in modern works on that subject are practically identical with those of three centuries ago.

Now there is good reason for believing that towards the end of the seventeenth century this Socinian literature really attracted much attention in England, and probably with considerable effect. But as a matter of fact no English translation of any part of it was made before John Bidle's propagandist activity in the middle of the century, and we have the explicit testimony of Bidle himself and most of the earlier Unitarians that they were not led into their heresy by foreign books. It was the Bible alone that made them unorthodox.

A famous illustration of this is the case of *John Milton* (1608-74). In 1823 a long-forgotten MS. of his was found in a State office at Westminster, and two years later it was published under the editorship of Dr. Sumner, afterwards Bishop of Winchester. The work is entitled *A Treatise of Christian Doctrine*. It was a late study by the poet, laboriously comparing texts and pondering them with a mind prepared to receive the verdict of Scripture as final, whether in agreement with orthodoxy or not.

The most ardent of Milton's admirers, and even the most eager Unitarian, must find the book a trial; but the latter can at least claim the author of *Paradise Lost* as an Anti-trinitarian, and the former may solace himself by noticing that here, as in all the rest, Milton's soul 'dwelt apart. ' He emphatically denies that it was the works of 'heretics, so called, ' that directed and influenced his mind on the subject. We may notice here the interesting fact that another great mind of that age, *Sir Isaac Newton*, has left evidence of his own defection from the orthodox view; and his correspondent *John Locke*, whose views appear to have been even more decided, is only less conspicuous on this point because his general services to breadth and liberality of religious fellowship are more brilliantly striking.

Locke's *Plea for Toleration* is widely recognized as the deciding influence, on the literary side, which secured the passage of the Toleration Act in 1689. Deferring for the moment further allusion to the position created by this Act, we must at once observe the scope of one of Locke's works which is not so popularly known. This is his *Reasonableness of Christianity*, which with his rejoinders to critics makes a considerable bulk in his writings. In pursuance of the aim to 'reduce the number of essentials' and to discover that in the Christian religion which is available for simple people—the majority of mankind—Locke examines the historical portion of the New Testament, and presents the result. Practically, this amounts to the verdict that it is sufficient for the Christian to accept the Messiahship of Christ and to submit to his rule of conduct. The orthodox critics complained that he had omitted the epistles in his summary of doctrine; his retort is obvious: if the gospels lead to the conclusion just stated, the epistles cannot be allowed, however weighty, to establish a contrary one. Of course, Locke was called a 'Socinian'; but the effect of his work remained, and we should remark that if it looked on the one hand toward the orthodox, on the other it looked toward the sceptics and freethinkers who began at that time a long and not ineffectual criticism of the miraculous claims of Christianity. Locke endeavoured to convince such minds that Christianity was in reality not an irrational code of doctrines, but a truly practical scheme of life. In this endeavour he was preceded by Richard Baxter, who had written on the 'Unreasonableness of Infidelity, ' and was followed during the eighteenth century by many who in the old Dissenting chapels were leading the way towards an overt Unitarianism.

III. THE OLD NONCONFORMISTS

The reader must be reminded here of a few salient facts in the religious history of the seventeenth century. All these undercurrents of heterodox thought, with but few and soon repressed public manifestations of its presence, were obscured by the massive movement in Church and State. During the Commonwealth the episcopal system was abolished, and a presbyterian system substituted, though with difficulty and at best imperfectly. After the Restoration of Charles II the Act of Uniformity re-established episcopacy in a form made of set purpose as unacceptable to the Puritans as possible. Thereupon arose the rivalry of Conformist and Nonconformist which has ever since existed in England. Severely repressive measures were tried, but failed to extinguish Nonconformity; it stood irreconcilable outside the establishment. There were distinct varieties in its ranks. The Presbyterians, once largely dominant, were gradually overtaken numerically by the Independents. Perhaps it is better to say that, in the circumstances of exclusion in which both were situated, and the impossibility of maintaining a Presbyterian order and organization, the dividing line between these two bodies of Nonconformists naturally faded out. There was little, if anything, to keep them apart on the score of doctrine; and in time the Presbyterians certainly exhibited something of the tendency to variety of opinion which had always marked the Independents. Besides these bodies, the Baptists and Quakers stand out amid the sects comprised in Nonconformity. In both of these there were distinct signs of Anti-trinitarianism from time to time; as to the former, indeed, along with the earlier Baptist movements in England and on the Continent (especially in the Netherlands) there had always gone a streak of heresy alarming to the authorities. Among the Quakers, William Penn is specially notable in connection with our subject. In 1668 he was imprisoned for publishing *The Sandy Foundation Shaken*, in which Sabellian views were advocated. It need hardly be pointed out that among the still more eccentric movements, if the term be allowed, heterodoxy as to the Trinity was easy to trace.

When the Toleration Act was passed the old Nonconformity became 'Dissent, ' that being the term used in the statute itself. Dissenters were now granted freedom of worship and preaching, but only on condition that their ministers subscribed to the doctrinal articles of the Church of England, including, of course, belief in the Trinity.

Unitarians, therefore, were excluded from the benefit of the Act, and the general views of Dissenters upon the subject are clear from the fact that they took special care to have Unitarians ruled out from the liberty now being achieved by themselves. Locke and other liberal men evidently regretted this limitation, but the time was not ripe, and in fact the penal law against Unitarians was not repealed till 1813. Unluckily, too, for the Unitarians, a sharp controversy, due to their own zeal, had broken out at the very time that the Toleration Act was shaping, and as this had other important results we must give some attention to it.

IV. THE 'UNITARIAN TRACTS'

There are six volumes, containing under this title a large number of pamphlets and treatises, for and against the new views, published about this period. It is the first considerable body of Unitarian literature. Its promoter was *Thomas Firmin*, a disciple of John Bidle, on whose behalf he interceded with Oliver Cromwell, though himself but a youth at the time. Firmin, a prosperous citizen of London, counted among his friends men of the highest offices in the Church, some of whom are said to have been affected with his type of thought. Apart from his Unitarianism he is remarkable as an enlightened philanthropist of great breadth of sympathy. Men of very different theological bent who were fain to seek refuge in London from persecutions abroad were aided by funds raised by him. We should notice also that, ardent as he was in diffusing Unitarian teachings, he had no wish at first to set up separate Unitarian chapels; his desire was that the national Church should include thinkers like himself. We are thus pointed into a path which for a time at least promised more for Unitarian developments than anything very evident in the Dissenting community.

The situation is aptly illustrated by a little book of 184 pages which is included in the first volume of the *Tracts*. This work is specially noteworthy as one of the first English books to use the name 'Unitarian, ' though the use is here so free and without apology or explanation that we must suppose it had already attained a certain vogue before 1687, the date of the book. The title is *A Brief History of the Unitarians, called also Socinians*. Neither author nor publisher is named, but the former is known to have been the Rev. Stephen Nye, a clergyman, whose grandfather, Philip Nye, was noted in his day as one of the few Independents in the Westminster Assembly. Stephen Nye's book takes the form of four Letters, ostensibly written to an unnamed correspondent who has asked for an account of the Unitarians, 'vulgarly called Socinians. ' The opening letter states their doctrine, after the model of Socinus—God is One Person, not Three; the Lord Christ is the 'Messenger, Servant, and Creature of God, ' also the 'Son of God, because he was begotten on the blessed Mary by the Spirit or Power of God'; 'the Holy Ghost or Spirit, according to them, is the Power and Inspiration of God. ' (We may notice here that Bidle, otherwise agreeing with Socinus, regarded the Holy Spirit as a living being, chief among angels.) Nye, writing as if an impartial observer, presents the Scripture argument in support of the doctrine of the Unitarians, 'which, ' says he, 'I have so related as not to judge or rail of their persons, because however learned and reasonable men (which is their character among their worst adversaries) may be argued out of their errors, yet few will be swaggered or chode out of them. ' He traces the doctrine to the earliest Christian times, and shows the stages of Trinitarian growth. Incidentally he says that Arian doctrines are openly professed in Transylvania and in some churches of the Netherlands, and adds that 'Nazarene and Arian Churches are very numerous' in Turkish, Mahometan, and pagan dominions where liberty of conscience is allowed. He mentions celebrated scholars who have 'certainly been either Arians or Socinians, or great favourers of them, ' such as Erasmus, Grotius, Petavius, Episcopius, and Sandius—the last-named a learned historian who had made a special point of collecting admissions by orthodox writers of the invalidity of all the texts in turn usually quoted in support of the Trinity. In the subsequent chapters Nye deals *seriatim* with such texts, and the book ends with a commendation from 'A Gentleman, a Person of Excellent Learning and Worth, ' to whom the publisher had sent it for remark.

Upon such levels the discussion proceeded, the skill and adroitness of the heretics contrasting with the obvious perplexity of the orthodox, who soon fell to accusing one another of stumbling into erroneous statements. Dons, deans, and even bishops joined in the fray, and some of them, notably Dr. Sherlock, Master of the Temple, got into sad trouble with their brethren. Finally, the clergy were forbidden to prolong the discussion, which indeed promised little satisfaction to any but the heretics who enjoyed the difficulties of the orthodox champions. The traditional formularies were there, and these must suffice. In the presence of the restrictions imposed by the Toleration Act speculation outside the Church turned towards 'Deism'—perhaps the best modern equivalent would be 'Natural Religion. ' Speculation inside the Church had to accommodate itself to the creeds and articles, and thus there grew up an Arianism among the clergy which was really largely diffused and produced some important books. One of these was Dr. Samuel Clarke's *Scripture Doctrine of the Trinity* (1712), a work which appears to have helped many a clergyman to ease his conscience while reciting the authorized Trinitarian expressions, though in substance his opinions were no less heretical than those for which men had suffered under the law.

A contemporary case of such suffering was that of *Thomas Emlyn* (1663-1711), an Irish clergyman who was sentenced at Dublin in 1703 to imprisonment which lasted for two years. This gross treatment, excited keen criticism at home and in the American colonies, whither our attention must soon turn. Emlyn was the first minister to call himself a 'Unitarian, ' but under the pressure of the times, and in accordance with the spirit of Clarke and the other Arianizing clergy, he found it expedient to declare himself a 'true Scriptural Trinitarian.'

V. THE OLD DISSENT

It is estimated that about a thousand Meeting Houses were erected by Dissenters in the twenty years following the passing of the Toleration Act. After the death of Queen Anne others were built, but in no great numbers. The prevailing impression of the state of religion in England during the first half of the eighteenth century is a gloomy one. Formalism and apparently an insincere repetition of the doctrinal phrases imposed by the law was but too evident in the State Church. Dissent had its bright features, but these grew dim as years went on. It must be admitted that the odds were heavy against that party. Without conforming no one could be appointed to public office, and the 'occasional conformity' of sharing the communion service at an established church now and again in order to qualify was at length forbidden by the Act of 1711. The sons of the Dissenting gentry and manufacturers were excluded from the universities, and though a shift was made by 'Academies' here and there, the excellence of the education they might impart could not compensate for the deprivation of the social advantages of Oxford and Cambridge. By an Act of 1714 schools for more than a rudimentary education were forbidden to be taught by Dissenters. Thus, we are not surprised to hear, considerable defection went on, and early in the century congregations began to dwindle. As it proceeded some became very small indeed, and many died out altogether.

The trusts upon which the Meeting Houses were founded were frequently free from any close definitions of the doctrines supposed to be held by the congregation. Much discussion arose in later years as to the purport of this freedom; perhaps there was some expectation of changing opinion in the future, but more probably the doctrinal status was taken for granted. It must be remembered that no Dissenting preacher could legally officiate without previously 'subscribing' to the doctrinal articles of the Church of England or their equivalents in the Westminster Assembly's catechisms. Thus, while the Dissenter might alter the terms of his liturgy to a degree not allowed to the Churchman (though the latter would in those lax days go pretty far sometimes), he was still supposed to be 'sound' on the fundamental creeds. It would appear to be a fortunate accident for Unitarian development in some of these old Dissenting congregations that, either the prevalent understanding or a hope for speedy inclusion in the national Church, or a prevision on the part of liberal-minded men here and there, left so largely undefined the basis of religious union among them, as congregations.

However that may be, it is certain that a degree of reluctance to 'subscribe' began to show itself, and this, we surmise, was often due to other reasons than liberality pure and simple. That there were broad-minded men who, while conscientiously orthodox themselves, refused to exclude unorthodox ministers from their fellowship is shown by a notable instance among the Baptists. Before 1700, Matthew Caffyn, one of their body, being charged with Anti-trinitarian opinions, was still retained in membership by vote of the General Baptist Assembly, this being the first instance of any organization's formal acceptance of latitude respecting the Trinity. In Ireland, deterred no doubt by the harsh punishment of Emlyn, there was natural hesitation in avowing such latitude; but in 1721 a division began in Ulster between those who insisted on 'subscribing' the creed anew and those who opposed; and a few years later the 'non-subscribers, ' being excluded from the Synod, formed a new Presbytery which in course of time became distinctly Unitarian. The historic event for English 'non-subscription' was a declaration made at a meeting of Dissenting ministers, Independents, Baptists, and Presbyterians, held in 1719 at Salter's Hall, London. Certain Exeter ministers had become unsound in doctrine, and refused to renew their subscription to the creeds and articles, claiming to believe 'the Scripture'—a well-understood expression in those days. The question of their exclusion was referred to London, and there again the point of renewed 'subscription' was raised before the vote on the Exeter case was taken. By seventy-three to sixty-nine it was decided that the declaration of faith should be confined to 'the words of Scripture'—as Sir Joseph Jekyll put it, 'the Bible carried it by four. ' This was widely recognized as setting open the door for liberty in matters of religion, and the interesting fact should be recorded that Independents and Presbyterians were found on both sides.

Here, then, we may for the present leave the English development; it was slow, tentative, for the most part obscure. In one direction and another the movement of thought might be perceived, in the Church, among the 'Congregationals, ' or Baptists, or Presbyterians, as the case might be. It was only long after that much preponderance of heretical opinion was distinctive of Presbyterian congregations. In the Academies men like *Philip Doddridge* (1702-51), the hymn writer, were affording room at least for ample discussion among the students, and moderate as his own opinions were he is credited with having made so-called 'orthodoxy' a byword. The Independents, Caleb Fleming and *Nathaniel Lardner* (1684-1768), led the way to 'Humanitarian' views, the latter being a learned writer of much influence. It is said that another great hymn writer, Isaac Watts, finally shared the Humanitarian view. On the whole, with some notable exceptions, the Dissenting preachers seem to have been decorously dull, and uninspiringly ethical. Without the zeal of the 'enthusiast, ' whom they severely scanned from afar, and seeking in all things to prove that Christianity was so 'reasonable' as to be identical with 'rational philosophy, ' it is little wonder that when the popular mind began to be stirred by a religious 'Revival' they were not its apostles, but mostly its critics. This is precisely the point where we may fitly turn to consider the growth of Unitarianism in New England.

NEW ENGLAND

I. BEFORE THE 'GREAT AWAKENING'

As in the Old Country, so in the colonies of North America, a great evangelical revival took place towards the middle of the eighteenth century. John Wesley the Arminian, and George Whitefield the Calvinist, were the great apostles of this movement, and the latter especially was very influential in America. The English revivalists were not alone, however; among the most powerful leaders in the colonies was Jonathan Edwards, whose name ranks very high in the records of religious philosophy in the States. Despite preliminary obstacles this preacher of the most stern and unflinching determinism produced a quite extraordinary effect at last. As usually happens, his dogmas were more easily repeated by others than his reasoning; violent excitement ran through the colonies, and it was this that gave a decisive turn to the liberalism which ultimately developed into a very memorable phase of Unitarianism. The preceding steps may be briefly indicated.

A familiar epigram preserves the acid truth that the Puritan emigrants who left England in the seventeenth century went to North America in order to worship God in their own way, and to compel everyone else to do the same. Religious liberty was certainly not understood by them as it is understood to-day. The sufferings of the Baptists and Quakers, for example, make a sad chapter of New England history. About the middle of the century, *Roger Williams* (1599-1683), having ventilated opinions contrary to the general Calvinism, was driven out of Salem, where he had ministered to a grateful church. His pleas for a real religious freedom were in vain, and he was forced to wander from the colonial settlements and find a precarious home among the Indians. After much privation, he succeeded in establishing a new colony at Rhode Island, where a more liberal atmosphere prevailed.

It does not appear that Williams had much influence in the general world of religious thought, but two things at least were favourable to the modification of orthodoxy. On the one hand there was inevitably a looser system of supervision in a new country, and the pressure of penal law could not be exerted so effectually as in England. On the other hand the organization of worship and teaching, though intended to be strict and complete, an intention fairly successful in practice, was actually founded upon broad principles. Each township maintained its 'parish church, ' but this, originally of a Low Church or 'Presbyterian' type, was usually accommodated as years went on to a Congregational model. These churches were looked upon as centres of religious culture for the respective communities by whose regular contributions they were supported and endowed. The 'covenants' by which the members bound themselves were often expressed in terms quite simple, and even touching; the colonists were in the main faithful to the parting injunction of the famous Pastor John Robinson, who sped the 'Pilgrim Fathers' on their way with the assurance that the Lord had 'more light and truth to break forth from His Holy Word. ' Occasionally, it is expressly declared by the covenanting members that theirs is an attitude of devout expectation of religious growth.

As would naturally be expected, the conditions of the earlier generations in the colonies were not in favour of a deeply studious ministry; the leaders were more frequently men of shrewd and practical piety than profound scholars. As things became more settled, and especially after the Toleration Act had secured a more assured state of feeling at home, the minds of men were set at liberty in a greater degree. Locke's works were carried across the sea, and Dr. Clarke's Arianizing writings soon followed. Apparently, the first stir of any importance was produced by the scandal of the punishment of Thomas Emlyn, the Irish clergyman who has been previously referred to. Emlyn's writings received a great advertisement, and although he managed, like Clarke, to avoid further legal difficulties by publishing a statement of his adherence to a 'Scriptural Trinity, ' his defection from the orthodox dogma was clear enough and his arguments against that dogma remained. Another case which was notorious in those days was that of *William Whiston* (1667-1752), the well-known translator of the works of Josephus, who was dismissed from his professorship at Cambridge in 1710 for Arianism. A prolific writer and a shrewd debater, Whiston played no small part in the general leavening of opinion.

But probably the most direct of the literary influences in this direction came from the pen of *Dr. John Taylor* (1694-1761), one of the most able and learned of the Presbyterian divines. His treatises on *Original Sin* (1740) and the *Atonement* (1751) dealt with subjects of the profoundest importance in relation to the usual Trinitarian scheme of doctrine. Preferring, for his own part, to be known by no sectarian name but to be reckoned among 'Christians only, ' Taylor was recognized far and wide as a writer extremely 'dangerous' to the ordinary type of belief. When the American revivalists were at their height, there were many quiet and staid New England ministers who found in Taylor a welcome ally against the extravagances which they witnessed and deplored. The more logical the Calvinist was, the more vivid in depicting the horrors of predestined damnation, the more vigorous these men became in denouncing such a doctrine. Perhaps the growing sense of individual liberty and personal rights had much to do with the reaction. A theory based upon the postulate of an absolute and unconditioned sovereignty divine did not accord with the growing democratic temper. Preachers began to insist, and hearers to agree, that, whatever 'salvation' is, it must be reasonable if reasonable creatures are to enjoy its benefits. Here also, as among the English latitude-men, the conviction grew that the essentials of a Christian belief must be few and simple and these such as plain men could understand and discuss; and here, as among the sober Dissenters at home, men looked askance on unintelligent outbursts of emotion.

The process of change was not very fast, and a good many who were sensible of change in their opinions were reluctant to accept new doctrinal designations. Arians they might be, but they preferred to be known as standing by a 'Scriptural Christianity. ' For, whatever new books might be written, the Bible remained their chief study and their support in discussion. Keen, rational rather than mystical, yet deeply interested in moral progress and human elevation, these American divines were much of a mind with their English brethren whose path lay in the same direction. One of the most influential preachers was *Charles Chauncey* (1706-87); who for sixty years was minister at the 'First Church, ' Boston. His theology was Arian and 'Universalist' (i. e. holding the doctrine of a final universal salvation); his Anti-Calvinism came out forcibly in his protests against the revivalist excesses. It is recorded of him that in his youth, disgusted by noisy fanatics, he prayed God never to make him an orator. His prayer was granted—and still he was a power!

II. THE LIBERAL REACTION

With the rise of the new liberalism in the American colonies no name is more conspicuous than that of *Jonathan Mayhew* (1721-66), whose eloquence was of a more modern type than most of his day. He is credited with having deeply moved many who became leaders in turn, whether as ministers or laymen. After the interruption of normal development inevitable during the War of Independence, things moved more rapidly. The French Revolution evoked the warmest sympathy in the United States, and its effect on religion there was largely to increase a sense of the worth of man. 'Universalism, ' the final restoration of all, became a conspicuous doctrine with some. The need for practical measures to uplift the general life here was a theme more to the mind of others. The distinctly 'Unitarian' trend was from the first associated with this eager attention to the higher culture. Harvard College, in the very heart of New England, rapidly developed into a fruitful source of the newer ideas, which were embodied in the lives of 'statesmen, merchants, physicians, lawyers, and teachers'; and thus the community, in all its more vigorous members, became charged with a fresh conception of life and religion.

In the first decade of the nineteenth century we begin to trace publications more or less distinctly Unitarian. One of these was the *Monthly Anthology*, the pioneer among American literary magazines. One of its two editors was the Rev. William Emerson, father of Ralph Waldo Emerson. As the divergence of ideas grew more distinct debate began to be fierce. The new magazine took a bold line, while many liberals were still hesitating. In 1808 the trouble came to the surface. Harvard was denounced by the orthodox party, in consequence of the appointment of a liberal minister, Henry Ware, to a professorship involving pastoral care of the students. An orthodox rival school was set up at Andover. A few years later a pamphlet appeared giving letters alleged to have been sent to England by Boston ministers reporting that a certain number were Unitarians. The name was unwelcome at the time, especially because it was associated with the 'humanitarianism' then becoming widely taught in England. The implicated ministers, being charged with cowardly evasion, replied with warmth; they were, in fact, mostly Arians, and thus their views really were different from the English type. Moreover, again in contrast with the English, they expressed strong dislike of controversy; all they asked was to be left alone to proclaim the 'Simple Christianity' in which they believed.

The upshot showed, however, that controversy was not to be avoided, and during twenty years from 1815 onwards it raged more or less severely. An epoch in this long and regrettable warfare was marked by a sermon preached at Baltimore in 1819. The preacher was one of the most famous men on the Unitarian roll, *William Ellery Channing* (1780-1842). Already eminent, he continued to hold a position unique in the religious life of New England; his saintly character and his noble if simple eloquence made him a leader in spite of himself. For a long time he had maintained a mediating position—all through his life he resolutely disclaimed sectarianism; but in 1819, after years of discussion, it was obvious that, for good or evil, the old dogma and the new spirit lay far apart. From that date liberals and conservatives in the old Congregational system of New England were divided, and 'Unitarian Christianity, ' which was the subject of Channing's discourse, was a recognized type in the land. In 1825 the American Unitarian Association was founded. It was but a struggling society at first, not for lack of sympathy with its principle, but because many Unitarians, like Channing, so strongly disliked the notion of forming a new sect that they took little interest in methods of propagandism common to most religious bodies.

ENGLISH UNITARIANISM RECOGNIZED BY LAW

By a mere coincidence the British and Foreign Unitarian Association was founded almost on the same day in 1825 as the American Unitarian Association. This step evidently implies a great change in Unitarian affairs since the times of that early Dissent towards which attention has been previously directed. We must now endeavour to trace the change in detail.

It will be remembered that tendencies to Anti-trinitarian thought — using that term to cover all the varieties of heretical opinion on the subject — were manifested both within the established Church and without. As regards the latter phase, the evidence is clear that, whatever the doctrinal 'subscription' was worth which Dissenting preachers had to make, there was a decided lapse from the orthodox standard on the part of a considerable number. This lapse, however, was for the most part left obscure while the pulpits resounded with 'plain, moral discourses. ' Now and again, one bolder than the rest ventured to discuss controverted points of doctrine. Such a man was *Joseph Priestley* (1733-1804), whose career is interesting as an illustration of the growth of opinion, and especially important in regard to the denominational advance of Unitarianism. He began life as a Calvinistic Independent, and became Arminian, Arian, and Humanitarian in turn. His devotion to science is well known, and he ranks with Lavoisier as an original discoverer of oxygen. He was an indefatigable student, a voluminous writer, a ready controversialist; and though his speaking was marred by imperfect utterance he attained to considerable influence in public address. No Unitarian leader hitherto has displayed more activity, and few, if any, have possessed greater controversial ability than he. His opinions, indeed, were in some respects peculiar to himself; he called himself a Socinian, but it was with a difference, and no Unitarian to-day would endorse some of his main positions. But his work for the cause was invaluable, and his personal character is held in the highest esteem. Originally he would have preferred that the Unitarians should remain as a 'liberal leaven' in the churches; eventually he became the chief organizer of Unitarian worship and propaganda.

The first 'Unitarian Church, ' however, was due to a clergyman, *Theophilus Lindsey* (1723-1808). After long and arduous efforts to secure relaxation from the doctrinal subscription imposed on the clergy, Lindsey resigned his living at Catterick, in 1773, facing poverty and hardship with a courage that elicited warm commendations, though few were found to imitate the example. In spite of the terrors of the law, now becoming a dead letter, he opened a Unitarian chapel in Essex Street, London, in 1774. The service was on the episcopal model, but with a liturgy adapted to 'the worship of the Father only. ' This feature has been claimed to be the distinctive characteristic of modern Unitarianism. It will be remembered that Socinus inculcated a sort of subordinate worship of Christ, and the Arians of course held to the same practice, Humanitarianism, the view that Jesus Christ was truly a man and in no sense a deity, obviously made it impossible to offer him the adoration due to God alone. This view had been slowly spreading since the days of Lardner; Priestley, Lindsey, and the active men of the party generally shared it. There were exceptions still, however. *Dr. Richard Price* (1723-91), a London Presbyterian divine of great eminence, remembered as one of the founders of actuarial science, held by his Arianism to the last; this did not prevent him from lending a hand in the organization of the Unitarian forces, but there was for a time some difficulty on the subject. The more ardent professors of the new doctrine of 'the sole worship of the Father' were for excluding the Arians from fellowship, and one of the societies then formed actually adhered to a rather offensive formula on the subject till about 1830.

A considerable number of liberal Churchmen of the laity, including some of rank, supported Lindsey's movement. An indication of changing moods is given in the fact that in 1770 an Act was passed permitting the Dissenting ministers to preach provided that they made a declaration of belief in the Scriptures as containing the revealed will of God. This was considered by many a welcome relief from the requirement of the Toleration Act that the minister must subscribe to the doctrinal articles of the established Church, and it was certainly a much less definite test. Priestley, for his part, however, regretted the change; the old subscription was in reality ceasing to be enforced, and he was afraid lest persecuting vigilance would set in again. As a matter of fact, the Act of 1779, long obsolete, has never been repealed, but very few people are aware of its existence. Priestley's many controversies tended to excite a good deal of interest, some of it more than unfriendly, in the new movement. In 1791, when a party of Unitarians dined at Birmingham in celebration of the French Revolution, serious riots broke out, and Priestley, who was then minister of the New Meeting there, was made a principal victim though he was not one of the diners. His house and library were burned, and he barely escaped the violence of the mob. Other residences were also destroyed, and the Old and New Meetings were burnt down. Ultimately, in 1794, Priestley sought asylum in America from the ill-will that pursued him even in London. Bishop Horsley, one of his sturdiest opponents in controversy, said, 'the patriarch of the sect is fled. '

It was earlier in the same year that the first organized Unitarian propaganda took shape in a *Unitarian Society for Promoting Christian Knowledge*. District unions were soon formed, and in 1806 a Unitarian Fund was raised by means of which the first itinerant missionary of the body, *Richard Wright* (1764-1836), was sent literally from end to end of Great Britain. In 1813, Unitarians were set free from legal penalties by the repeal, so far as they were concerned, of the exceptive clauses of the Toleration Act, this relief coming twenty years after Charles James Fox had tried to secure it for them. The member who was successful was Mr. William Smith, who sat for Norwich, and whose granddaughter was Florence Nightingale. In 1819 an Association was founded to protect and extend the Civil Rights of Unitarians. It was by combining the three societies—the Society for Promoting Christian Knowledge, the Fund, and Civil Rights Society, that the British and Foreign Unitarian Association was formed, as has been said, in 1825.

In order to understand fairly the scope and spirit of that earlier Unitarian period, thus at last organized in full legal recognition, though still suffering from the prejudice inevitably created by more than a century of legal condemnation, a few salient points should be kept in view. First, the heterogeneous elements in the 'body, ' if it could be called such, were a source of weakness in regard to united action. Instead of belonging, as their American brethren did, to one ecclesiastical group, and that the dominant one, the English Unitarians included Dissenters of different tendencies and traditions, with a few recruits from the State Church. The 'Presbyterian' congregations, as they were not very strictly called, were the backbone of the 'body'; many of these, however, were very weak, and in the course of a few decades some were destined to follow those which had died out in the eighteenth century. Converts not infrequently lent new force in the pulpit, but at the risk of substituting an eager missionary spirit for the usual staid decorum of the old families. In these the ideals of breadth, simplicity, and moral excellence were stronger than the desire, natural in a convert, to win the world to one's opinion.

Again, it must be borne in mind that then, as generally, there were men whose thoughts ran ahead of those of the majority. Priestley, for example, while adhering to the idea that the Christian revelation had been guaranteed by miracles, had abandoned belief in the Virgin birth as early as 1784, and went so far as to maintain that Jesus was not impeccable and had certainly entertained erroneous ideas about demoniacal possession. Probably there were very few who had arrived at these conclusions even thirty years later; some Unitarians repudiated them at a much later period. The miraculous element, however, was formerly accepted by all. So was the authority of Scripture, though here again men like Priestley were ahead of the rest in bringing to the study of the Bible the principles of historical criticism. *Thomas Belsham* (1750-1829), a typical Unitarian scholar and divine at this period, was one of several who carried forward the science of Biblical interpretation, and by the use of a vigorous and fearless intellect anticipated views of Genesis and the Pentateuch which did not find general acceptance till much later.

It is customary for Unitarians themselves to-day to look back on these years of early zeal and controversy with but a qualified sympathy, so much was still cherished in the body as a whole that is no longer tenable, and again so much that was undreamed then is indispensable to modern thought. One of the greatest of Unitarians, Dr. Martineau, whose important share in the development of their ideas and life must be considered farther on, referred in a discourse of about forty years ago to three distinct stages in Unitarian theology. First, he pointed to the significance of the struggle for the principle of 'Unity in the Divine causation, ' as against a doctrine which, as Unitarians maintain, endeavours in vain by words to prevent a triplicity of 'Persons' from sliding into a group of three Divine Beings. This struggle marks in great part the whole track by which the reader has come thus far in the present story. The second stage, according to Dr. Martineau, is that in which the Conscience of Man is emphasized, in virtue of the belief in a real responsibility and an actual power to choose the right or the wrong. This 'Religion of Conscience' he sees especially illustrated in the principles enunciated and the work accomplished by Channing; perhaps it would be fair to say that many who had preceded the American leader were imbued with a measure of his wisdom when they insisted, as we have seen, on the adaptability of the pure Gospel message to the needs and understanding of men everywhere, and declared that its aim was 'to make men good and keep them so. ' The third stage, which Dr. Martineau considered to be fully begun at the time of his sermon (1869), is that of the 'Religion of the Spirit, ' in which the ideas of the Divine Sovereignty and the Human Duty are rounded into vital beauty and completeness by the idea of the actual relation of Man to God as a Son to a Father.

We have referred in advance to this compendious view in order to show whither the sequel is to lead us, but before this all-important development can be traced there remains one more piece of external history to be supplied. Happily it may be dealt with summarily.

QUESTIONS OF INHERITANCE

The bitterness of theological discussion which troubled the earlier decades of the nineteenth century received new provocation in the shape of litigation about property. Both in England and America the right of Unitarianism was challenged to hold those Meeting Houses and Parish Churches respectively, to which allusion was made in our opening pages. In New England the chief matter of contention was settled as early as 1818. In the Old Country the struggle was much more protracted, and was only brought to an end by special legislation in 1844.

The American dispute may be briefly stated. In consequence of the growing and unconcealed departure of the liberal Congregationalists from the doctrinal standards of the past there arose a feeling among the conservatives that the former group should go out of fellowship, but the communal conditions of the parish made this out of the question. All the citizens had a right to share in the provision for religion which was made at the general cost. An acute difficulty, however, presented itself in regard to the choice of minister. Should he be of the orthodox or the heterodox type? The appointment being for life made an election most critical. An incident of this kind occurred at Dedham, Mass., and coming into the courts led to a decision in favour of the liberals, i.e. of the 'Unitarianizers. ' The case was argued in this way: A majority of members on the register being in favour of one type, are they at liberty to choose as they will? Or have the citizens at large, being contributories to the maintenance funds, a right to vote? It was decided by the courts that the popular right was valid as against the wishes of any inner and covenanted group of worshippers. This meant, in substance, that orthodox voters were outvoted by heterodox voters who had not enrolled themselves by a religious pledge. The chagrin of the defeated conservatives was naturally great, and harsh language ensued. The upshot was unaffected, of course, and time alone has had to soften the angry feelings which for a long time kept the two wings of New England Congregationalism hostile, to the regret of good men on each side. In recent years very friendly relationships have been happily set up, while the Unitarians remain undisputed heirs of the old Parish Churches. It should be carefully noted, however, that in 1833 the communal support of religion was abolished, and all religious bodies in the United States have been dependent since then upon private resources.

In England the orthodox opponents of Unitarianism tried to oust the heterodox congregations of the old Meeting Houses. A suit for possession of endowment funds which was finally decided against the Unitarians of Wolverhampton began in 1817; and a strongly organized attack followed in 1825. A rich fund for ministerial support, Lady Hewley's Charity, was, after actions carried to the highest court, declared not to be applicable to the assistance of Unitarians. This decision, in 1842, looked like the beginning of the end for the tenure of the Meeting Houses themselves, the Wolverhampton case being now decided on the lines of the Hewley judgment. But an Act of Parliament—the *Dissenters' Chapels Act*— passed in 1844 (owing in some part to the powerful support of Mr. W.E. Gladstone), secured the congregations in undisturbed possession. The principle of this law applies to all places of worship held upon 'Open, ' i. e. non-doctrinal Trusts; where the congregation can show that the present usage agrees substantially with that of the past twenty-five years, it is not to be ejected. At the time of this litigation the term 'English Presbyterian' came much into vogue among Unitarians, and for some time there was a marked abatement of propagandist zeal.

MODERN UNITARIANISM

I. THE COMMUNITIES

Having now followed the fortunes of the Unitarians up to the point where they obtained a recognized position among religious organizations, we need not enter into the minute details of their denominational history. Less than seventy years have elapsed since the passing of the Dissenters' Chapels Act, and less than a century since the judgment in the Dedham case. The congregational increase, though substantial, has not been great; Unitarians claim rather to have influenced the advance of thought in other denominations than to have created one more sect. At present their numerical strength may be estimated from the following particulars.

In the British Isles and colonial centres there are nearly four hundred places of worship, and a similar number of ministers; in many cases the congregations are small, and the list of ministers includes some that are retired and others who are regarded as 'lay-workers' only. There are about five hundred ministers and congregations in the United States. Two or three colleges in England and a similar number in America train students for the ministry, but many join the ranks from other denominations. Women are eligible as ministers, but actual instances are rare. Local unions exist to a fairly adequate extent. In England and America National Conferences meet at intervals; the Unitarian Associations continuously publish literature, send out lecturers, and promote new congregations. There are several periodicals. The most noteworthy in England is the *Hibbert Journal*, which follows in the line of other reviews of high standard in past years, and which specially illustrates the spirit animating a large and influential section of the body. It is promoted for free and open intercourse between serious thinkers of all schools of theological and social philosophy, and is reported to have a circulation quite beyond that of any similar publication. The 'Hibbert Lectures, ' connected with the trust founded in 1847 for the diffusion of 'Christianity in its simplest and most intelligible form, ' further exemplify the broad interpretation of this duty. Scholars of different churches have contributed to the series of volumes well known to religious students. The principle followed in general is stated in the oft-quoted phrase—'Free Learning and Free Teaching in Theology. '

It is needful, perhaps, to guard against the inference that the Unitarian movement is only, or in the main, an intellectual one. Since 1833, in consequence of a visit by *Dr. Joseph Tuckerman*, from Boston, 'Domestic Missions' were founded, to promote the religious improvement of the neglected poor, and to-day this kind of work still goes on with much social benefit in our larger cities. Similar benevolence has marked the American side. Many congregations, too, are composed largely of working-people, and in recent years a Van Mission has carried the Unitarian message into the country villages, mining districts, and other populous parts. These aspects of their activity are apt to be obscured owing to a pardonable disposition of Unitarianism to point to the 'great names' associated with their churches. In the American list, for example, we find Emerson, Longfellow, O.W. Holmes, Bryant, Hawthorne—Whittier and Lowell had close affinities; Bancroft, Motley, Prescott, Parkman; Margaret Fuller, Louisa Alcott; and statesmen, jurists, merchants, and scientists too numerous to set down here. Obviously, the English side cannot rival such a brilliant roll; the *élite* of society has not been here, as in New England, on the side of the newer theology. Yet English Unitarianism has its eminent mimes also, alike in literature, science, politics, philanthropy, and scholarship of various kinds; and the body is credited with a civic strength out of proportion to the number of its avowed adherents, while its philanthropies have been of the same broad and enlightened kind as those which enrich the American record.

II. IDEAS AND TENDENCIES

More important to the general public is the question of ideas which now prevail among Unitarians. Our preceding sketch has shown some of the results of the freedom claimed by them in one generation after another. We have now to see in what respects the nineteenth century effected a further change.

In the first third of the century there can be no doubt that Unitarians adhered tenaciously, but with discrimination, to the idea of the final authority of the Bible. In this respect they were like Protestants generally, and though they nevertheless brought 'reason' to bear on their reading of the Scriptures, other Protestants did the same, if to a less degree. Both in the United States and in England this attitude was still common up till nearly the middle of the century, and instances could easily be found later still. The miraculous element was thus retained, though as we have seen as early as in Priestley's case there was a tendency to eliminate some part of the supernatural. That a thoroughgoing belief could be stated in good round terms is evident from the following sentence taken from a book issued by *Dr. Orville Dewey* (1794-1882), one of the most eloquent pulpit orators of his day. The book is entitled *Unitarian Belief,* its date is 1839. Referring to the Bible the author says, 'Enough is it for us, that the matter is divine, the doctrines true, the history authentic, the miracles real, the promises glorious, the threatenings fearful. ' There is good ground for taking this as a fair example of the ideas prevalent among American Unitarians at that time. Perhaps the statement was made the more emphatic in view of some remarks recently uttered by two young men whose influence, along with more general tendencies, proved fatal to the old doctrine.

One of these young men was *James Martineau* (1805-1900), who at the age of thirty-one was already known as a writer and preacher far above the average. He was then resident in Liverpool, where he wrote a remarkable little book with the title *The Rationale of Religious Inquiry* (1886). More than fifty years later he published an even more remarkable book, *The Seat of Authority in Religion.* There is, indeed, half a century of development between the two books, yet the germinal thought of the second may be detected in the first. The point at issue is where the ultimate appeal should lie in matters of religion. With the keen eye for the weaknesses of his fellow-worshippers which always characterized him, Martineau said, 'The

Unitarian takes with him [to the study of the Bible] the persuasion that nothing can be scriptural which is not rational and universal. ' This fixed opinion, which he ranks along with the foregone conclusions of other types of theologian, was just that which we have observed in the general course of liberals from Locke onwards. Though in a note Martineau concedes that his words may somewhat strongly accentuate the common opinion, he represents Unitarians as virtually saying, 'If we could find the doctrines of the Trinity and the Atonement, and everlasting torments in the Scriptures, we should believe them; we reject them, not because we deem them unreasonable, but because we perceive them to be unscriptural. For my own part, I confess myself unable to adopt this language'—not, he says, but that he does think them actually 'unscriptural. ' 'But I am prepared to maintain, that if they were in the Bible, they would still be incredible.... Reason is the ultimate appeal, the supreme tribunal, to which the test of even Scripture must be brought. ' It abates nothing from the force of these declarations that then, and for some time afterwards, Martineau himself accepted the miracles. The 'old school' perceived the sharp edge of such a weapon, and its wielder was during many years regarded as a 'dangerous' innovator.

The other young writer to whom reference has been made was *Ralph Waldo Emerson* (1803-82), son and grandson of ministers of the liberal Congregational type in New England and himself for a short time minister of the Second Church, Boston. Preferring the freedom of the lecturing platform, Emerson had already withdrawn from the ministry, but in 1838 he gave an 'Address to the Senior Class' in the Divinity School, Harvard, which proved a second landmark in the history of American Unitarianism. Nineteen years before, Channing had decisively pointed out that Unitarianism and orthodoxy are two distinct theologies. In the Divinity School Address, Emerson maintained that the idea of 'supernaturalism' is rendered obsolete by a recognition of the reality of things. Bringing a gift of pungent prose to the service of a poetic imagination, Emerson startled the decorously dignified authorities of the New England pulpit; he 'saved us, ' says Lowell, 'from the body of this death. ' He pointed from the record of miracles past to an ever-present miracle. To the illumination of 'reason, ' which Unitarians had followed so loyally— within the proviso of a special revelation—he brought the light of a mystic intuition. Some of his elders judged it to be 'false fire' perilously akin to the 'enthusiasm' which their predecessors had so often condemned. In daring simplicity he urged that there had been 'noxious exaggeration about the *person* of Jesus. ' 'The soul knows no persons. ' The divine is always latent in the human. Revelation is not ended—as if God were dead!

The shock to the old-fashioned minds was immense. Long and far-sounding debate followed, though Emerson, with provoking self-possession, declined to argue. He simply 'announced. ' This oracular attitude certainly affected some of the younger men greatly, but fortunately for the success of the new gospel one of these younger men translated the oracular into a more popular and reasoned form. Three years after Emerson's Address, *Theodore Parker* (1810-60) completed the Unitarian trilogy by a sermon on *The Transient and the Permanent in Theology*. It may be said to have done for Emerson's message the kind of service rendered by Huxley to Darwin's. Parker at once became a marked man; most Unitarian pulpits were closed against him, but a large hall accommodated the vast crowds that came to hear him. It is doubtful if such numerous congregations ever listened to a Unitarian before or since. He continued an arduous work for some fifteen years, but it wore him out before his time. He was an erudite scholar and a prolific writer. Discarding the claims of Christianity to be the only 'divine revelation, ' he based his clear and always optimistic theism on the broad facts of human experience. Ardently interested in social and political questions, he poured satire without stint on the religious defenders of slavery, and himself dared all risks along with the foremost abolitionists. Such a man could not but count for much; and though his radical views in theology greatly disturbed for many years the conservatives in the body—for Unitarianism itself had by this time a well-defined conservative type—they could not fail to permeate the minds of the masses.

Of Emerson's own life-work this is hardly the place to speak at large, but in connection with the development of that 'Religion of the Spirit' in which Dr. Martineau sees the culmination of the theological progress of Unitarianism, Emerson's share must be allowed to be a large one. When Dean Stanley visited America he is said to have reported that he had heard sermons from many pulpits, but 'Emerson was the one preacher in them all. ' It is certain that at one time the style, if not also the thought, of Emerson was extensively copied by the preachers, not always to the gain of solidity. A degree of jauntiness appears in the worse specimens of these imitations, and Lord Morley's criticism that Emerson himself was too oblivious of the dark side of human suffering and guilt would doubtless apply to much of the Unitarian eloquence at one time inspired by his witching voice.

This, however, is but one side of the American message in the nineteenth century; evidence abounds that a 'Christocentric' type of teaching, with adhesion to much of old material of the Gospels, held its own till a generation ago, and its peculiar accent is not without echoes to-day. On the whole it is probable that, as at the beginning of the century, the 'liberals' in New England Congregationalism were somewhat shocked at some of the daring views of the Priestleyan Unitarians in England, so even towards its close the general position of thought was more conservative there than was the rule here. Certainly, also, there was a deep, tender tone manifested even where opinion was most radical among the American Unitarians, and of this no better proof can be cited than the large number of hymns of a high order both of thought and expression which have been written among them. They serve to show that a frank acceptance of the evolutionary philosophy by no means necessarily entails the decay of devout personal piety or the loss of beautiful ideals. Among the American hymnists the following are specially eminent, and their productions are often to be found in 'orthodox' collections: *Samuel Longfellow* (brother to H. W.L.), *Samuel Johnson, W. C. Gannett, J. W. Chadwick,* and *F. L. Hosmer.*

On the English side other sweet singers have appeared: 'Nearer, my God, to Thee, ' by *Sarah Flower Adams*, is a world-renowned hymn; and if the names of Channing, Emerson, and Parker cannot be equally matched here in their several spheres, there has been no lack of able and scholarly representatives, and one name at least is of universal reputation. That name, of course, is *Martineau*. The effective changes from the old Unitarianism to the modern type are best displayed in the story of his long life and the monumental books which bear his name. Reference has been made to his early brilliance; its promise was amply fulfilled in the course of a career more than usually prolonged. The note of original thought sounded in the *Rationale* (see p. 63[*]) was to be heard again and again in other and more permanent utterances, and not seldom to the perplexity and dismay of many of his Unitarian brethren. Alike in religious philosophy, in attitude to the Scriptures, and in matters of church organization, he found himself from time to time at variance with most of those close around him. His philosophical and critical influence was in large measure victorious; in regard to organization the results were less satisfactory to himself. It will be instructive to observe his progress.

[*: third paragraph of Modern Unitarianism: II. Ideas and Tendencies.]

As regards philosophy, it is necessary to remember the influence of Priestley and Belsham. These Unitarian leaders, following Hartley's psychology, stood for a *determinism* which was complete. God was the Great Cause of all; not the 'First Cause' of the deistic conception, operative only at the beginning of the chain of events and now remote from man and the world, but present and immediate, exhibiting his divine purposes in all the beings created by him. Christianity, in the view of this school, was the means by which God had been pleased to make known the grand consummation of this life in a perfected life to come; Jesus, the Messiah, was the chosen revealer of the divine will, and his resurrection was the supreme and necessary guarantee that his message was true. Martineau, like the rest of his generation, was brought up in this necessarianism; but its tendency, as he reviewed and tested it, was to do violence to certain irrepressible factors of the spiritual life. It is only fair to say, there was even in this Priestleyan school room for a mystical mood; but on the whole it appeared dry and intellectual, lacking the warm and operative forces of a deeper devotion.

It is interesting to find that Martineau himself confessed that the freshening touch upon his own inner life came in a closer contact with evangelical piety. His mind was to the end of his many years readily responsive to congenial impulses, let them come whence they would, and no small part of his service to Unitarianism consists in the broader sympathies which he generated in its circles. To Channing, also, he expressed gratitude for helping to wake in him a new sense of the meaning of life and religion. It was Channing's characteristic to insist on the significance of personality. The worth, the depth, and also the rights of the Human made so vivid an appeal to his mind as to react on his conceptions of the Divine. Within, a few years after the *Rationale* was published, Martineau is found making an obvious change of base. He has realized that the externally communicated religion of the old school, however sublime in its proportions, fails to meet the needs or, indeed, to fit the facts of the inner life. Man's personality rises, in his thought, into touch with God's; the revelation from without can only be recognized as such by the aid of a revelation within; a real activity, a genuine moral choice, and a resulting character, the marks of a truly living Soul, these are indispensable to an adequate view of the religious life. But all this involves two significant positions, each far asunder from those hitherto put forth—there must be Freedom, at least in the moral world; and the Divine assurances of moral values and of loving aid to win them are no longer confined to an outer record. Such a record may yield invaluable service as a heightener and interpreter of individual experience; to the last we find Martineau attaching a profound and quite special significance to the revelation in Jesus of the life of sonship to God, and retaining tenaciously the Christian attitude in preference to one of simple theism. But his system is based on the internal; all the rest, the Church, the Bible, Nature, however august and charged with meaning, is supplementary to that.

In the American field, under the influence of Emerson and the German philosophy, what is called 'Transcendentalism' flourished midway in the century, and there as well as in England its extravagances were deplored. Martineau himself, while approaching so nearly to the egoistic centre, was safeguarded from all such vagaries by an all-pervading sense of duty. In his volumes of sermon the *Endeavours after the Christian Life*, and *Hours of Thought on Sacred Things*, which remain among the choicest of their kind in our language, his austerity of moral tone is only relieved by an elevation of poetic mysticism till then unknown in Unitarian literature. It was, indeed, his conviction that the body would not write poetry for a generation or two, so dry and prosaic did he find it; but at that very time his own efforts in hymnody on one side and on the other his lyric prose, almost too richly ornate for general wear, were touching new springs of feeling. By and by, he issued in conjunction with others a set of liturgical services, which did much to lend dignity to congregational worship. And what gave unique influence to his ideas was his intimate connection from 1840 to 1885 with 'Manchester College, ' London, one of the successors to the old 'Academies' (now after its several migrations handsomely housed at Oxford). At this college, as professor of mental and moral philosophy and for many years as Principal, he made a deep and lasting impression on the minds of most of the leading scholars and preachers. His great works. *Types of Ethical Theory* and *A Study of Religion*, gathered up the harvest of long study and exposition in these subjects, and are the most important of their kind given by Unitarians to the world.

In accordance with what has been indicated, the later attitude of Martineau, and naturally of his pupils—though the principle of free and independent judgment is and always has been insisted upon—has been radical in respect to Biblical, and especially to New Testament, studies. An influence in this department more direct than his own was formerly found in the writings and lectures of *John James Tayler* (1797-1869), his predecessor as Principal. This ripe and fearless scholar brought home to Unitarians the wealth of continental literature on the subject. The 'old school' stood aghast as the tide of 'German criticism' overflowed the old landmarks of thought; and when Tayler himself issued a work strongly adverse to the apostolic authorship of the Fourth Gospel distress was extreme. In these matters, however, the tide proved irresistible, and the next generation of preachers and students were among the most ardent translators and popularizers of the new views of Jewish and Christian origins. The 'free' character of the pulpits has made the way easier than in most other denominations for the incoming of modern thought in this and other directions.

The influence of natural science upon the trend of Unitarian opinion has hardly been second to that of Biblical criticism. Some names in the list of prominent Unitarians are celebrated in this connection—*Louis Agassiz* (1807-73), for example, on the American side, *Sir Charles Lyell* (1797-1875) and *Dr. W.B. Carpenter* (1813-85) on the English side. A son of the last named, *Dr. J. Estlin Carpenter*, a man of wide and varied scholarship, is now Principal of Manchester College. A field in which he is specially expert is that of comparative religion, and here also is a source of many considerations that have transformed Unitarianism into one of the most liberal types of thought in the modern religious world.

It is not to be inferred, however, that the 'radical' tendencies, while predominant, have everywhere prevailed among Unitarians. The 'conservative' side continued in the third quarter of the nineteenth century to yield important signs of its existence and fruitfulness, and its vitality is far from exhausted still. The miraculous element has even here been reduced to a minimum, but it has left a tinge on the picture of Jesus which fills the imagination and kindles the reverent affection of many. Among the more gifted representatives of this school we may name the Americans *Dr. H.W. Furness* (1802-96) and *Dr. J. Freeman Clarke* (1810-88), and the English *John Hamilton Thom* (1808-94). Thom's sermons are ranked among the highest for spirituality and penetration; they certainly had profound effect in stimulating the wise and generous philanthropy of *William Rathbone* and *Sir Henry Tate*. A celebrated representative of this side of Unitarianism is *Dr. James Drummond*, still living, the author of several works of European repute among New Testament scholars, one being a defence of the Johannine authorship of the Fourth Gospel. He succeeded Martineau as Principal of Manchester College. His volume. *Studies of Christian Doctrine*, is the most important statement of the Unitarian view published in recent years.

As time went on, it fell to Martineau and other leading Unitarians to take up a defensive attitude against the extreme forces of negation. In particular, he came to be recognized as a champion of theism against materialist evolution. Four volumes of 'Essays' contain some of his acutest writings on the subject. An address presented to him on his eighty-third birthday celebrated his eminence in this and other ways; it bore the signatures of six hundred and fifty of the most brilliant of his contemporaries, at their head being Tennyson and Browning.

All this strenuous progress, however, was for Martineau dogged by a shadow of peculiar disappointment. In youth he was as ardent a 'Unitarian' as any; but, about the time of the Dissenters' Chapels Act (1844), he and Tayler and some others felt increasing dissatisfaction with the tendency of the more active Unitarians to degenerate into a sect. As we have seen, the same divergence of feeling arose in America, and Channing always strove to keep Unitarianism there from succumbing to denominationalism. The ardour of those especially who had newly espoused the Unitarian view and found it precious to themselves may be easily understood, and they might be forgiven some impatience with the apparent apathy of those who had no great desire to multiply proselytes. Some of these eager spirits strove to rescue the body from what they evidently regarded as a paralysing indefiniteness. From time to time it was argued that Unitarianism must be 'defined' authoritatively; then, and then only, might a triumphant progress be secured. Mixed with such notions was apparently a desire to keep the imprudent and 'advanced' men from going 'too far. ' In one form or other this opposition has persisted till the present; but its acrimony has sensibly lessened as, on the one hand, the 'denominational' workers have more fully accepted the principle of unfettered inquiry, and on the other, the lessons of experience have shown that, however eager the Unitarians may be for the widest possible religious fellowship, they are, in fact, steadily left to themselves by most of the other religious bodies, especially in this country. Martineau himself about forty years ago tried to form, along with Tayler, a 'Free Christian Union' which should ignore dogmatic considerations; but Tayler died, and so little encouragement was met with outside the Unitarian circle that the thing dropped after two years. Nearly twenty years later, at the Triennial Conference (held in 1888 at Leeds), a remarkable address was given by the now venerable 'leader' (whom, as he mournfully said, no one would follow), in favour of setting up again an English Presbyterian system which should swallow up all the many designations and varieties of association hitherto prevailing among Unitarians. The proposal was considered impracticable, and the dream of a 'Catholicity' which should embrace all who espoused the free religious position, whatever their doctrines, seemed farther than ever from fulfilment. In later years the idea has, however, continued to be mooted, and some Unitarians hope still to see the development of a 'Free Catholicism' in which the traditional distinction between Unitarian and Trinitarian will be lost.

Meanwhile, as has been said, the extension of Unitarian worship and the diffusion of literature goes on with a fair amount of success. In America, thanks largely to the sagacious toil of a remarkable organizer, *Dr. H.W. Bellows* (1814-82), the Unitarian Association has proved a strong and effective instrument for this purpose, and the British Association, whose headquarters are now in the building where Lindsey opened the first Unitarian Church in 1774, has also thriven considerably in recent years. It is said that the rate of growth in the number of congregations in the United Kingdom has been about 33 per cent during the past half-century; in America the rate is somewhat higher.

III. METHODS AND TEACHINGS

It will not be surprising to the reader to learn that a religious body having such a past and being so variously recruited to-day is far from stereotyped in method. At the same time there is practical agreement on the main lines of doctrine.

In worship different forms are used. Many churches have liturgies, adopted at discretion and usually supplemented by free prayer. In others the free service alone is preferred. Lessons are chiefly taken from the Bible, but selections are sometimes read from other devotional literature. Several hymnals have wide acceptance; a few are peculiar to single congregations. The large majority of sermons are read, though extempore address is now less infrequent than formerly. 'Sacraments' are not considered indispensable, but the Lord's Supper is retained in many cases and is regarded as a memorial. The baptism (or 'dedication') of infants is also practised.

Ministerial ordination is not considered as imparting supernatural gifts, but as a solemnity marking the entrance of the accredited person into full recognition and office. The congregation makes its own choice of a minister, though in case of its dependence upon outside financial assistance the advice of the managers of the Fund may be offered. The support of the churches and Sunday-schools, etc., is generally by voluntary contributions; endowments exist in some instances. Church membership is usually granted without insistence upon any religious declaration. New buildings are invariably associated with the 'open trust' principle, the way being thus left open for such changes in worship and opinion as may hereafter seem right. Some churches decline to be known as 'Unitarian, ' and where that name is adopted it is usual to find with it the explanation that this does not pledge or limit future development or bar the widest religious sympathy in the present.

Reference has been made to Sunday-schools. In this field Unitarians have always been pioneers, and their aims have usually been to promote culture without sectarian zeal. Many large schools continue, as in the past, to form centres of education of the widest type, not only to children but adults. Much interest is taken in social amelioration; some observers have asserted that this interest is more vivid in many quarters than any in matters theological or philosophical.

Unitarianism

Statements of the teachings usually accepted in the churches are numerous. One here quoted will fairly represent the general type. It was drawn up by *Richard Acland Armstrong* (1843-1905), an eager social reformer, a powerful preacher and author, and memorable especially as a popularizer of Martineau's religious philosophy. Of course, from what has been already said, such a statement is not regarded as an authoritative creed, but simply takes its place as one out of many summaries for popular diffusion.

'Unitarian Christianity teaches that God is our Father, full of love for all of us. It learns from Jesus that the Father listens to our prayers and watches over us with even more tender care than over the lilies of the field and the birds of the air.

'It learns from Jesus too, that however important it may be to have correct views concerning religious matters, it is much more important to love God with all our heart and mind and soul and strength, and our neighbour as ourselves. For he says that these are the first two commandments, and that there is no other whatever that is greater than these.

'It learns from Jesus, also, that the way to enter the kingdom of Heaven is, not merely to hold a correct theology or to receive any outward sacraments, but to "be converted and become as little children"—simple-hearted, loving, pure.

'Unitarian Christianity teaches that God our Father claims us all as children, and that when Jesus speaks of himself as God's Son, he means us all to remember that we are God's children too, though unhappily we have stained our sonship and daughterhood with many unworthy thoughts and deeds.

'Unitarian Christianity loves the Parable of the Prodigal Son, because it shows so clearly and so beautifully the love and forgiveness of God, and with what tender pity he looks on us when we have sinned.

'Unitarian Christianity believes that God speaks to his children now as truly as he did to the Prophets of old and to Jesus Christ, comforting, strengthening, enlightening them. Conscience itself is his holy voice.

'Unitarian Christianity sees in Jesus Christ a supremely beautiful life and character, a marvellous inspiration for us all, an ideal after which we may strive; and it loves to think of him as our Elder Brother, of the same nature as ourselves.

'Unitarian Christianity does not believe that God will plunge any of his children into everlasting woe. Such a thought of God is a contradiction of his Fatherhood. He is leading us all, by different ways, towards the pure and holy life for which he brought us into being.'

Along with this may be taken the declaration adopted, as a result of somewhat protracted discussions, at the National Conference of Unitarians in America, 1894; it would probably be accepted in all similar assemblies.

'These churches accept the religion of Jesus, holding in accordance with his teaching that practical religion is summed up in love to God, and love to man; and we invite to our fellowship any who, while differing from us in belief, are in general sympathy with our spirit and our practical aims.'

UNITARIANS AND OTHER RELIGIOUS LIBERALS

The broadly sympathetic spirit which has been observed at work in the foregoing story has led to interesting relationships between Unitarians and some other religious bodies. The Universalists, who are strongest in the United States, are cordially fraternal with them; and a large proportion of the 'Christians'—a non-dogmatic body— are equally close in sympathy. The Hicksite Friends, named after Elias Hicks, who early in the nineteenth century avowed Anti-trinitarian views, and some other religious bodies less conspicuous are more or less directly included in the Unitarian forces, though not organically in union. With the French Liberal Protestants there has been warm co-operation for many years, and the same is true of Dutch, German, and Swiss reformers. Since the visit of Rammohun Roy, the Indian reformer, in 1833, the English in particular have developed kindly relations with the Indian theist movement, and students from India and Japan are regularly educated at Oxford for the ministry of free religion in their own countries. It is in this way, more than by the ordinary types of missionary activity, that Unitarians have hitherto attempted to influence the non-Christian races.

During recent years there have been held international congresses promoted by the Unitarians of Great Britain, America, and Transylvania, and attended by representatives of the various sections just named as well as by others from the orthodox churches, including Anglican and Romanist, who venture to brave the authorities thus far. Proposals have already been made for a world-wide union of Religious Liberals, in view of the remarkable success of these great congresses; but the circumstances of the different groups, especially in Germany and Holland, seem to forbid expectation of such a development within any near period. On the whole, Unitarians appear to be encouraged by the signs of the times, and to do their share of religious culture and benevolent work while cultivating the friendship of 'Modernists' of all kinds, Christian, Jewish, Moslem, and Hindoo.

CHRONOLOGY

1536-1612. Many trials and executions for denying the Trinity; notably *Servetus* (1553); four East Anglians, 1579-89; Legate and Wightman, 1612.

1568. Francis David founds the Unitarian Church in Hungary.

1578-1604. Faustus Socinus active in Poland.

1595. The Racovian Catechism. Other Socinian works follow.

1640. Canon against Socinian books in England.

1644-62. John Bidle's career.

1646 and onward. Anti-trinitarians among Baptists, Independents, Friends, etc. Books against 'Socinianism. '

1662. Act of Uniformity—ejection of Nonconformists.

1674. Milton d., leaving his *Treatise of Christian Doctrine* in MS. ; discovered 1823 and published.

1687. Stephen Nye's *Brief History of the Unitarians*, etc.

1689. Toleration Act—Unitarians excluded.

1689-97. The 'Unitarian Controversy. ' Being suppressed, 'Arianism' developed among clergy, 'Deism' among other writers.

1690. Presbyterian Academy (now College, Carmarthen) founded.

1695. Locke's *Reasonableness of Christianity*.

1700. General Baptist Assembly accept Anti-trinitarian membership.

1703. Thomas Emlyn imprisoned for denying the Trinity.

1719. 'Non-subscription' vote at Salter's Hall, London.

1740. Arianism diffused; Humanitarianism incipient.

1742. The 'Great Awakening' revival in New England, followed by a Liberal reaction.

1755-1804. Joseph Priestley's career.

1774. Theophilus Lindsey's Unitarian Chapel, London.

1786. Manchester Academy (now College, Oxford) founded.

1790+. Unitarian propaganda active in England.

1808. Controversy in New England Congregationalism.

1813. Toleration Act extended to Unitarians.

1817. Proceedings begun against Unitarians in respect of inherited Chapels, etc.

1818. The 'Dedham Case, ' Massachusetts.

1819. Dr. Channing's 'Baltimore Sermon. '

1825. Founding of Associations in Great Britain and U. S.A.

1836. Martineau's *Rationale.*

1838. Emerson's *Divinity School Address.*

1842. Theodore Parker's *Discourse.*

1844. Dissenters' Chapels Act.

1847. Hibbert Trust founded.

1854. Unitarian Home Missionary Board (now College, Manchester) founded.

1882. National Triennial Conferences begun.

1890. Martineau's *Seat of Authority.*

1900. International Congresses founded.

AUTHORITIES

R. WALLACE. *Anti-trinitarian Biography*, 3 vols., Lond., 1850.

A. GORDON. *Heads of English Unitarian History*, 1 vol., Lond., 1895.

J. H. ALLEN. *Unitarianism since the Reformation*, 1 vol., New York, 1894.

J. J. TAYLER. *Retrospect of the Religious Life of England*, 1 vol., Lond. (3rd Ed.), 1876.

W. G. TARRANT. *Story and Significance of the Unitarian Movement*, 1 vol., Lond., 1910. (Gives more detailed references.)

For statistics and special characteristics of the various Liberal Religious bodies in general accord with Unitarians see the following records of the International Congresses: —

Liberal Religious Thought at the Beginning of the Twentieth Century. Ed. by W. COPELAND BOWIE, Lond., 1901.

Religion and Liberty. Ed. by P. H. HUGENHOLTZ, jun., Leyden, 1904.

Actes du III'me Congrès International du Christianisme Libéral et Progressif. Ed. by E. MONTET, Geneva, 1906.

Freedom and Fellowship in Religion. Ed. by C. W. WENDTE, Boston, 1907.

Fifth International Congress of Free Christianity and Religious Progress. Ed. by WENDTE and DAVIS, Berlin (and London), 1911.